MW01173024

Name:

Date:

All Scriptures in Preface are NASB. All Scriptures in the rest of the book are NIV unless otherwise noted.

Disclaimer: All names in personal stories throughout this book are changed for purpose of anonymity.

ISBNs
Print or paperback ISBN: 978-1-7362393-3-9
Kindle ISBN: 978-1-7362393-0-8
eBook ISBN: 978-1-7362393-1-5
Print or paperback ISBN, 2nd Edition: 978-1-7362393-5-3
Kindle, 2nd Edition: 978-1-7362393-4-6
Print workbook: ISBN 978-1-7362393-6-0

Permission requests:
Contact Greg Williams at loveandlordship@gmail.com or 859.229.6504.

Ordering information:
For bulk orders or quantity discounts, contact Greg Williams at loveandlordship@gmail.com or 859.229.6504. Includes any ministry or faith-based organization that would like to partner with us to sell books for 20% of net profits.

Printed in the United States of America.

February 2023

GREG & AMI WILLIAMS

THE
AUTHORITY
OF
LOVE

WORKBOOK

Living in God's Covenant Design

INTRODUCTION

This workbook has been designed, in conjunction with *The Authority of Love, Second Edition* book to aid you in your walk and maturity in Christ in line with God's Covenant Design and Order. We must start with our own life and personal walk, and in our most intimate relationships…marriage and family as applicable.

With this in mind, we designed this workbook for individual, small group, and class or larger group studies, in order to reach and help as many as possible become disciples of Christ who make disciples of Christ in their homes, churches and beyond.

As we strengthen our discipleship walk in Christ we create healthy relationships, marriages and families, which build a more vibrant and flourishing Bride of Christ, His Church. Stronger homes and churches will give us a much greater impact in our culture and world as we advance His Kingdom. After all, loving relationships are the currency of His Kingdom and we must take that to heart as Christ's disciples.

While I'm excited about His Love & Lordship in each of our lives, I know this is a challenge that can only be fulfilled as you surrender fully to Christ.

Love & Lordship is a ministry that calls those who claim Christ as Savior and Lord to display the image of God in these four standards in their life and relationships:

1) Christ as Lord in all things reflected in…

2) Loving Marriages/Families/Relationships that lead to…

3) Relational Servant-leadership first in marriages and families and develops…

4) Generational Discipleship in personal life, family, The Church, and culture.

We want to encourage and challenge those who will take this to heart to allow it to drive them to Christ, His Spirit, and His Word, and into a relationship with Him as Lord and relationships with all others that reflect His Love.

My hope and prayer is that your knowledge of the Bible and your personal relationship with Jesus and His Holy Spirit will grow exponentially as you continue with us through the Love & Lordship series and message. I know that as you grow through this study it will positively change your life, marriage, family, and legacy, and in so doing, impact His Church and Kingdom and this culture through you.

At Love & Lordship, our desire is to help you live joyfully and have fulfilling relationships in the Love and Lordship of Jesus Christ. This message has changed hundreds of marriages and thousands of lives for His Kingdom and Glory!

This ride will cost you…but it's well worth it. So, strap yourself in and be prepared to become all that God has created and Christ has recreated you to be as you take the next steps in His Love and Lordship.

— Greg Williams

CONTENTS

AUTHORITY AND LOVE

Key Concepts

- True Authority comes from The Author – God, The Father, Son, and Holy Spirit.
- The world defines and practices authority as control or lording over others.
- Christ, The Author, defines and models relational servant-leadership as authority.
- Authority as relational servant-leadership begins in the marriage and family.
- Authority in Christ's Church is to be an extension of good leadership in the home.
- The world's authority prioritizes production, results, and success over people.
- True Authority prioritizes people and relationships over outcomes and success.

Authority and Love – A Real Life Story

Recall the story of Dennis in the beginning of the book (Chapter 1, p. 3, Print edition).

> ### *What is Love and Authority?*
>
> God, in His Word, has much to say about authority and love. Both are necessary to build Godly relationships that _____ His image and glory and that are healthy and fulfilling.

Authority and The Author

In God's Kingdom Love and Lordship (authority) are never _____ .

Lordship is authority or _____ and love is a _____ , right?

What do you think of when you hear "authority?"

Often the first answer is, "Police," followed by "Courts, government," and "boss, manager, and superior."

When we come across the word "authority," many of us immediately think in terms of control, supervision, management, or ruling/_____ over others. That's _____ authority.

Why is Authority important?

Authority should point us to the _____ .
The Author is the one who has, defines and
gives authority.

The Author is God, The _____ ; God, The _____ ; God,
The Holy Spirit, and He has revealed Himself to us in His _____ , The Bible.

Knowing the Author means we define and determine everything according to
His _____ .

> *"Our God is a covenant-making and covenant-keeping God and every covenant has an order."*
>
> — Dr. Tony Evans.

God has defined Authority and Love. Recognizing God as Author means we choose to live
with Him as Lord and walk in His Covenant _____ .

Why Love and Lordship? These are two of the most used and talked about words—yet
very few in our culture and world today know their true meaning and application.

You know who does? The Author! Why not look at what He says about Love and Lordship
so we can be grounded and rooted in True Authority and Love.

God and Christ as The Author

God is the Author, therefore we should _____ to Him as Authority. His Word is _____ and is lived out in the Order (principles and priorities) of His Design.

If we are convicted that we are living according to God's plan and Word, then we will be encouraged to stand _____ and keep the _____, individually and collectively.

Scriptures regarding God's Authority placed in Christ...

⇨ In **Matthew 28:18**, *Jesus said, "All authority has been given to me." By whom? The answer is: God the Father gave it to him.*

⇨ **Matthew 11:27** - *All things have been handed over to me by my Father, and no one knows the Son except the Father, and no one knows the Father except the Son and anyone to whom the Son chooses to reveal him.*

⇨ **John 3:35** - *The Father loves the Son and has given all things into his hand.*

⇨ **John 13:3** - *Jesus, knowing that the Father had given all things into his hands, and that he had come from God and was going back to God...knelt down and washed the apostles' feet.*

⇨ **Ephesians 1:20–21** - *God raised him from the dead and seated him at his right hand in the heavenly places, far above all rule and authority and power and dominion, and above every name that is named, not only in this age but also in the one to come.*

⇨ **John 17:2** - *Father, the hour has come; glorify your Son that the Son may glorify you, since you have given him authority over all flesh, to give eternal life to all whom you have given him.*

⇨ **Philippians 2:9-11** - *Therefore God exalted him to the highest place and gave him the name that is above every name that at the name of Jesus every knee should bow, in heaven and on earth and under the earth, and every tongue acknowledge that Jesus Christ is Lord, to the glory of God the Father.*

> *"I am determined to be absolutely and entirely for Him and for Him alone."*
>
> — Oswald Chambers, *My Utmost for His Highest*

Why Authority? Let's Just Love One Another

Authority affects _____ , whenever and however it is rightly or wrongly expressed.

Authority is _____ . Authority is _____ . What if we're doing it all wrong? As Christ followers we are taught that authority is completely _____ .

We say authority is humbly serving others. Let's look at how most people lead—in vocation, church, home, or in positions of authority—there is a very familiar pattern.

That pattern looks a lot like the 12 apostles that Jesus picked who argued to sit on the thrones in His Kingdom in Matthew 20. If it showed up in Jesus' handpicked disciples how much more likely are we to struggle with authority?

The first and greatest command speaks to God's Authority...

Mark 12:29-31 begins with, *The most important one, answered Jesus, is this: 'Hear, O Israel: The Lord our God, the Lord is one.'*

Before Jesus talks about love and its importance, He echoes what God told Moses in Deuteronomy 6:4-5.

God is alone, The _____ and _____ , worthy of our praise and _____ . Every person hearing Moses and Jesus proclaim this would have understood that the priority _____ begins with honoring God as Lord, as The Author, The One with All Authority. Jesus knew this in receiving His authority from The Father, in Matthew 28:18: *Then Jesus came to them and said, 'All authority in heaven and on earth has been given to me.'*

Recognizing Christ as Author(ity) impacts how we love and build relationships—especially marriage and family—and how we grow His Church and advance His Kingdom to influence the culture.

Scripture depicts only two places where authority is defined: The _____ (Ephesians 5:21-33) and the _____ (Christ's Family), and it is to follow that order (1 Timothy 3:4-5). All other authority in God's Kingdom flows from these.

Teaching True Authority

The foundational teaching in Scripture on authority: Matthew 20:20-28

The disciples are fighting over who will " _____ " (worldly authority) with Christ when He sits on the throne in His Kingdom.

It is not this way among you, but whoever wishes to become great among you shall be your servant, and whoever wishes to be first among you shall be your slave; just as the Son of Man did not come to be served, but to serve, and to give His life a ransom for many. - Matthew 20:26-28

There is great temptation in fallen humanity to want to "lord over" _____ .

Real _____ comes from a humble, submissive, servant heart.

Christ's teaching is very clear: those who truly lead are those who humbly place others above self and serve without _____ anything in return.

Controlling "authority" may work in this world but Kingdom authority is humbly serving others. When we choose to "lord it over" others we _____ our true authority.

The Essence of True Authority – Humility in Love

What is Humility in Love?

Humility is being _____ and _____ in who you are so you choose to put others above self.

Jesus knew that the Father had put all things under his power, and that he had come from God and was returning to God. - John 13:3

For by the grace given me I say to every one of you: Do not think of yourself more highly than you ought, but rather think of yourself with sober judgment, in accordance with the faith God has distributed to each of you. - Romans 12:3

For we are God's handiwork, created in Christ Jesus to do good works, which God prepared in advance for us to do. - Ephesians 2:10

Modeling True Authority

Jesus not only taught us what True Authority was, He _____ it!

When he had finished washing their feet, he put on his clothes and returned to his place. "Do you understand what I have done for you?" he asked them. "You call me 'Teacher' and 'Lord,' (TRUE AUTHORITY) and rightly so, for that is what I am. Now that I, your Lord and Teacher, have washed your feet, you also should wash one another's feet. I have set you an example that you should do as I have done for you. Very truly I tell you, no servant is greater than his master, nor is a messenger greater than the one who sent him. Now that you know these things, you will be blessed if you do them. — John 13:12-17 (parentheses added and mine)

Authority in God's Covenant Order

True Authority in The Home

For the husband is the head of the wife as Christ is the head of the church, his body, of which he is the Savior. — Ephesians 5:23

Wives, submit yourselves to your own husbands as you do to the Lord. — Ephesians 5:22

Submit to one another out of reverence for Christ. — Ephesians 5:21

True Authority in Christ begins in the most _____ of relationships—marriage, family, and the home. Husbands, before we ever claim any authority in our marriage and with our wives, and wives before we try to feign any submission toward our husbands, we should note Christ's example (John 13:1-17) and heed the verse above: "Submit to one another out of reverence for Christ."

True Authority in Christ's Church

He must manage his own family well and see that his children obey him, and he must do so in a manner worthy of full respect. (If anyone does not know how to manage his own family, how can he take care of God's church?) — 1 Timothy 3:4-5

Only two Roles of _____ are defined in Scripture: 1) Home 2) Church...

Fail to servant-lead in our homes and we will struggle to find it in Christ's Church or anywhere else.

> The qualities of a True Kingdom Leader (elder/overseer) in Christ's Church hinge on 5 key elements:
>
> 1) Godly character and integrity;
> 2) Able to teach and shepherd others;
> 3) Relational servant-leader (manager) in the marriage and family (absence of this negates leadership in His Church);
> 4) Humble maturity in the faith and;
> 5) Have a good reputation in the community.

True Authority in The World

Jabez was more honorable than his brothers... *Jabez cried out to the God of Israel, "Oh, that you would bless me and enlarge my territory! Let your hand be with me, and keep me from harm so that I will be free from pain." And God granted his request.* - 1 Chronicles 4:9a, 10

_____ and servant-leadership (True Authority) go hand in hand in Scripture, and yet there is a conspicuous absence of defining any 'leaders' in Scripture except for in the Home and Church. God wants us to learn to lead (<u>serve</u>) in the relationships where the most is at stake.

> John Adams, Founding Father and the Second U.S. President stated, ***Public virtue cannot exist in a nation without private, and public virtue is the only foundation of republics.***

We should heed God's Word and seek _____ from our marriages, families, homes, and from Christ's Church! They will lead in His Kingdom in this world.

The Rest of The Story

Refer back to *Dennis' story... "God's way is much better than mine."

God (Father, Son, and Holy Spirit) is the Author. His Truth, His Love and Lordship, is the only way to live our lives to the fullest.

> *"If our motive is love to God, no ingratitude can hinder us from serving our fellow man."*
>
> — Oswald Chambers, *My Utmost for His Highest*

NOTES

SECTION 2

THE STORY OF TWO KINGDOMS

Key Concepts

- Whoever is your Lord/lord or authority defines your Truth/truth.

- There are only two Kingdoms and therefore two Kings/kings (Lords/lords).

- Truth is Absolute and the Foundation for all things.

- Lordship is based on Absolute Truth and is inherent in all of life/relationships.

- Your choices reveal the priorities in your life.

- Priorities reflect who/what is in control of your life.

- All sin and problems in life come from rebellion against His Lordship and failure to recognize and live His Truth.

- Christ's example shows us that authority is invited influence rather than demanding, manipulating, or controlling.

- Humility and Integrity are essential in all healthy lives and relationships.

The Kingdom and Lordship of Christ

> *"Temptation usually comes through a door that's been deliberately left open."*
>
> — Scottish Theologian Arnold Glasgow (1905 – 1998)

Recall the story of *John from Chapter Four, p. 17, Print edition.

Christ as Lord

Christ is The Authority in God's Kingdom…over all of creation."

Then Jesus came to them and said, 'All authority in heaven and on earth has been given to me.' - Matthew 28:18

After Jesus said this, he looked toward heaven and prayed: 'Father, the hour has come. Glorify your Son, that your Son may glorify you. For you granted him authority over all people that he might give eternal life to all those you have given him.' - John 17:1-2

Jesus knew that the Father had put all things under his power, and that he had come from God and was returning to God. - John 13:3

Lordship determines _____ …how we will handle every issue in our lives and relationships.

Every struggle, sin, or issue you deal with stems from who is your _____ / _____ . Most of the time we only deal with symptoms that occur in the latter two and think we have resolved them.

The enemy's greatest deception is, "You are _____ of your own fate. You don't need a lord."

He's simply appealing to our natural desire to be in authority, in _____ .

Another of Satan's greatest _____ is to lure us away from The Author, redefine God's Truth according to our fleshly desires.

Case in point: Dr. Gary Chapman, author of *Five Love Languages*, states, "Love is the most important word in the English language—and the most confusing."

Because we've fallen for the lie that "love" is whatever we want it to be in making us feel good and fulfilled, it's all rooted in _____ , personal desire, and satisfaction.

Paraphrasing NASA, "Church, we have a problem!"

How do we solve this problem? God has the answer.

Authority and Truth

The most important word in any language is God's "capital T" _____ !

Lordship and discipleship reveal everything about your life and what you believe.

TRUTH LANGUAGE – Contrasting God's Truth and The World

WORD	WORLD	TRUTH
Love	"If it feels good, do it"	_____
Humility	Humiliation	_____
Authority	Dictate, control, "lord over"	_____
Integrity	Reputation over Character	_____ , _____
Discipleship	No "lord" needed	_____

The False Kingdom

The Serpent's Deception - You Can Be Lord of Your Own Life

Satan knew that God had given us free choice from the beginning, and that is where he got mankind to fall. This is the source of every sin in our lives and world today and throughout history.

Satan can't stand God and tries desperately to dethrone Him—but he can't.

Yet God has given him an eternal Kingdom that completely contrasts Christ's.

Satan does all that he can to get us to believe that we don't need a lord, which means we don't need to be anyone's disciple.

Christ calls us to be His _____ and make disciples for Him. Jesus calls us to be His " _____ - _____ ."

Who's Your Lord/lord? – Satan's Greatest and Only Deception

Satan's deception is _____ the same – Genesis 3:1-5

1) _____ – "Did God say…?" Do you really know God's Truth?

2) God's a _____ – "You won't die."

3) Satan's lie to us - "You will be like _____ / _____ ."

Only Two Kingdoms, Two Kings, Two Lords

It's this simple: there are only two _____, which means there are only two _____ / _____ Lords. You and I are not one of them.

There is only God's/Christ's Kingdom of _____ and Life, and Satan's kingdom of death and _____. You and I do not have a kingdom.

In light of this, it's even more important to know what God says… _____ _____, so you can know Him and know that you belong to His Kingdom.

The bottom line: Don't be _____ . Know Christ as Lord and know His Truth. He came and died for you to make that possible.

Deception and Relativism – Consent Replaces Covenant

Recall the story from the book (p. 27) shared with prisoners and addicts about stealing and porneia (our "truths") and how we choose our own truths and ignore God's.

> *Consent is a bad substitute for covenant and commitment.*

Path to The Fall and Sin

1. _____ "What did God really say…?" Do I know His Truth?
2. _____ "Surely you won't die." Do I fall for subtle lies?
3. _____ "You must not touch it." Relativism feeds the appeal of the flesh.
4. _____ "Pleasing to the eye and desirable for gaining wisdom." Satisfy the flesh (senses/emotions/selfish desires rule rather than God's Truth).
5. _____ "She took some and ate it … and he ate it." Please the senses (self).
6. _____ /_____ "They realized they were naked… made coverings for themselves." Now trapped in their sin they must cover it up.

Whoever is Lord/lord in your life _____ your every motive, thought, decision, action, and relationship.

Antithesis: Every motive, thought, decision, action, and relationship reveals who is Lord/lord of your life.

Genesis 3:1-11 – The enemy's _____ of Adam and Eve is still ours today.

Who's Lord/lord of your life? Knowing Christ as Lord and His Truth makes all the difference when the subtle lies and temptations come from the enemy.

It's a matter of life and death—and eternity!

In the world, authority is demanded, manipulated, about control, "lording it over" others.

In God's Kingdom, authority is _____ _____ in the lives who willingly surrender.

Return to the printed book to read the rest of *John's story (p. 29).

> *"Is Jesus Christ Lord of your experiences, or do you try to lord it over Him? Is any experience dearer to you than your Lord? He must be Lord over you, and you must not pay attention to any experience over which He is not Lord. There comes a time when God will make you impatient with your own experience —"I do not care what I experience; I am sure of Him."*
>
> — Oswald Chambers, *My Utmost for His Highest*

NOTES

DISCIPLESHIP: RESPONSE REQUIRED

Key Concepts

- Salvation is free and places us in a relationship with God we could have in no other way.

- Discipleship requires commitment and a cost on our part and makes Christ Lord.

- Christ as Lord means that He must take first priority in every part of our life.

- Being a disciple of Christ requires that I die to my own selfish interests.

- Honorable submission, honest surrender, holy sacrifice, and humble service characterize the life of a disciple of Christ.

- As Christ's disciple I'm called to sacrifice my life to Him.

- Discipleship requires by willing submission that I practice personal and relational disciplines found in God's Word and by the power of His Holy Spirit.

- A disciple of Christ practices and creates habits/disciplines in his life that allow him to live wisely and build good relationships in Christ and by The Holy Spirit.

- Discipleship is first and foremost about knowing, loving, and serving God so that we can then love and serve our fellow man.

Discipleship: Responding to Your Lord

> *If Christ is Lord of all and you claim to be in a relationship with Him, but He is not Lord of your life, then who is? If He's not Lord of your life, then what is your relationship with Him?*

The ONLY _____ we can be in a relationship with Christ is with Him as Lord.

_____ discipleship is not perfection; it is lifelong maturation.

Everyone has a Lord or lord; you are someone's _____ .

Every part of your life _____ who is your Lord or lord.

Scripturally, discipleship is _____ , not just knowledge or learning-based.

Personal discipleship requires obedience and _____ to God's Word in a loving relationship with Christ as Lord.

Relational discipleship is _____ and holding each other accountable to obedience as we share and apply His Word in loving relationships with others as Christ's disciples.

Recall "A Discipleship Story" from Chapter 8, p. 35, Printed edition.

Jesus on The Cost of Discipleship - Luke 14:25-35

Jesus requires that He takes first priority in your life over everything else.

The most important of relationships – marriage and family – are secondary only to Christ.

Consider Christ's examples of finances and commerce (building a tower) and battle strategy (army of 10,000) to reinforce the two sides of discipleship:

1) Commitment – wholehearted devotion to Christ as Lord is the cost of discipleship.

2) Ridicule – any half-hearted attempt at faith makes our discipleship a laughingstock.

This is the cost of discipleship...In the same way, those of you who do not give up everything you have cannot be my disciples. (Luke 14:33)

If we are not His disciples, then how can we claim that He is our Lord?

Four key priority principles for your personal development as His disciple:

1) Honorable _____ — Ephesians 5:21

2) Honest _____ — Galatians 6:7-9

3) Holy _____ — Romans 12:1-3

4) Humble _____ — John 13:1, 3

Sacrifice your _____

Ultimately the discipleship life calls us to _____ our SHAPE:

*S*piritual gifts. *H*eart/passion. *A*ptitude/ability. *P*assion/heart. *E*xperience/education. (from *Purpose-Driven Life*, Rick Warren).

Four key elements from John 13 for discipleship and relationship:

1) Love – Jesus showed them His _____ and _____ love (v. 1).

2) Humility – He knew He was from God, returning to God, and God had placed all things in His hands (authority) (v. 3). This is the essence of humility, being _____ and content in who you are in Christ so you can place others above yourself.

3) _____ /Servant's heart – Jesus got up from the table, removed His robe and put a towel around His waist and began to wash the disciples' feet (vv. 4-5).

4) Authority – After _____ Jesus, out of love, humility and service, calls attention to one thing...He is the Authority and this is Authority.

> *In one loving act of humble service and with one question and statement (vv.12-13), Jesus powerfully tells His disciples, then and now, that love, humility, a servant's heart, and authority cannot be _____ in His Kingdom!*

He finishes by describing discipleship, Do as I have done for you and you will be blessed. (vv. 14-17). Live as a humble _____ of your Master.

Discipleship calls us to follow His example in our lives and relationships for His Kingdom and Glory.

Each element is repeated in principle in the beautiful condensed Gospel story and our call to imitate Christ in Philippians 2:

_____ love and a humble servant's heart (6-8);

Our _____ call to be like Him (vv. 3-5);

_____ and authority (vv. 9-11).

Mature disciples in Christ (Romans 12:1-2) move from…

Young, immature believers, "Here's what I'm going to do for You!"

Mature followers of Christ, *"Here am I, do as you please in and through me."*

Practical Application: Living as Christ's Disciples

Recall the story of Greg overdoing it in preseason conditioning – passion without discipline (Chapter 10, p. 45, Print edition).

Two _____ elements for discipline and maturity…
1) Manageability; 2) Commitment.

_____ and _____ are inseparable in His Kingdom and defined by commitment.

> *Make it manageable so you can keep your commitment.*

9 Spiritual Disciplines of a Christ Follower

All of the following Scriptures were (should be) received as commands to all who were (are) disciples and love The Lord (***If you love me you will keep (obey) my commands.*** John 14:15)

Personal Discipleship Applications

The first six applications are for personal discipleship:

1) Bible Study – Spend time _____ in God's Word…2 Timothy 2:15; Deuteronomy 6:4-7; Colossians 3:16a

2) Prayer – Spend time daily in conversation with and _____ to God… Philippians 4:6; 1 Thessalonians 5:17; Ephesians 6:18 – For a simple process to remember when praying, try C.A.T.S. (*C*onfession; *A*doration/praise; *T*hanksgiving; *S*upplication or requests for self and intercession for others)

3) Quiet Time, Reflection, Meditation – Spend time _____ about what you're reading and praying about so you can know God more fully…Psalm 46:10; Psalm 19:14. Also read Psalm 19 and 119 during your Bible Study time.

4) Communion and Fellowship – Spend time growing in the discipline of communion with Christ (1 Corinthians 11:23-26) and in loving _____ with other believers (Acts 2:42)

5) Sabbath – Recognize and be _____ to the Sabbath principle that serves two purposes: 1) Recognize that God is Holy and we are not; 2) Recognize in our unholiness and weakness the need to rest and put aside pride in our own strength...Genesis 2:2-3; Exodus 20:8; Mark 2:27

6) Fasting – While not specifically commanded, this is a powerful _____ and physical discipline with great results...Acts 13:2, 14:23; Mark 9:29

These next three spiritual applications help us grow in relational discipleship with other Christ followers as we glorify God:

7) Worship – God alone is worthy of our personal and corporate worship and praise... Exodus 20:3-7; Deuteronomy 6:5; Luke 4:8; John 4:24

8) Giving/Serving – Discipleship results in an overflow in our love for God and love for others through sacrificial giving and service...2 Corinthians 9:6-8

9) Fellowship/Loving Relationships/Church – As we mature, both personally and relationally, as Christ's disciples by the power of His Holy Spirit in the disciplines of His Word and Spirit, we become more like Christ. Acts 2:42; Hebrews 10:24-25

These disciplines come together in the building up and fellowship of Christ's Church.

Discipleship in loving relationships builds our faithful testimony which to reach a lost and hurting world with His message... Matthew 28:18-20

> *Without discipline there are no disciples and no discipleship! Without The Holy Spirit we have no spiritual discipline.*

BEGIN WITH 5 MINUTES DAILY (manageable)...DON'T MISS A DAY (commitment)! Adjust time as needed. Let God grow you in your commitment to Him.

The Next Step: Discipleship

Recall Greg's story at the end of Chapter 10, p. 50, Print edition.

How might you apply (and tweak) these principles in your discipleship walk?

> *"If we are devoted to the cause of humanity, we shall soon be crushed and broken-hearted, for we shall often meet with more ingratitude from men than we would from a dog; but if our motive is love to God, no ingratitude can hinder us from serving our fellow men…no matter how men may treat me, they will never treat me with the spite and hatred with which I treated Jesus Christ. When we realize that Jesus Christ has served us to the end of our meanness, our selfishness, and sin, nothing that we meet with from others can exhaust our determination to serve men for His sake."*
> — Oswald Chambers, *My Utmost for His Highest*

A Judgment Day Parable: Lordship, Discipleship, and Relationship

Small Group Discussion (15 minutes) – What did you sense God saying to you regarding Christ's prophecy in Matthew 7:21-23 and the Judgment Day vision from the book?

Every relationship will reflect whether He is Lord of your life or not. You can be assured that He is and that He is blessing you to be a blessing to others as you serve Him and them. That's how discipleship is lived out – in loving relationships.

NOTES

RELATIONSHIPS...
WHAT WE WERE CREATED FOR

Key Concepts

- Discipleship is lived out in Relationship...with Christ and with others.

- Loving relationships are the currency of Christ's Kingdom.

- Either people or things are sacrificed, depending on how we are approaching and building relationships for His Kingdom or for ourselves.

- Lusts of the flesh, lusts of the eye, and pride of the mind all destroy relationships.

- Porneia is the greatest destroyer of loving relationships as it is the greatest expression of lust.

- Hesed/Agape is the sacrificial, selfless love of God that is given to us and allows us to love in return.

- Agape and porneia (or any pride/lusts) cannot willingly coexist. One will eventually win out in your heart.

- The Cookie Jar is an analogy of discipline, relationship, love, and lust.

- Love is a commitment, a choice, and an act of our will lived out in intentional investment in the lives of others.

- God's love is a full-orbed love as seen in healing the leper and in speaking tough Truth to the rich young ruler.

- God's love is lived out according to His Covenant Order in the priorities of relationships.

> *"The answer lies in a personal relationship to Jesus Christ... We can ever remain powerless, as were the disciples, by trying to do God's work not in concentration on His power, but by ideas drawn from our own temperament. **We slander God by our very eagerness to work for Him without knowing Him**... This is your line of service — to **see that there is nothing between Jesus and yourself. Is there?**"*
>
> — Oswald Chambers, *My Utmost for His Highest*

Disguising Godly Relationships

Recall Section 4 intro story of Craig Gross of XXX Church and Greg's sharing at IronMan (p. 60, Print edition).

The Currency of Christ's Kingdom: Loving Relationships

How are we doing when it comes to building loving relationships as His disciples—first in our homes and families, and then in His Church?

The currency of this world is _____ (stuff/pleasure/success). Matthew 6:24

The currency of God's Kingdom is loving _____ . Ephesians 4:2; 1 Peter 4:8; John 15:12-13, 17

> *The currency of Christ's Kingdom is loving relationships, nearly always built at the expense of the stuff of this world! What are you investing in...people or stuff?*

Our discipleship response to Christ must be _____ in relationship with Christ as Lord and in love with others.

The greatest destroyer of relationships is _____ (Greek) – sexual immorality of any kind rooted in fleshly lusts, desires, and idolatry (Galatians 5:16-21).

Loving Relationships vs. Stuff/Success

God's Word calls us to seek His Kingdom and Righteousness _____ (Matthew 6:33) and to focus on that which is eternal rather than temporal (2 Corinthians 4:18).

Three things that exist on this temporal earth that are Kingdom in nature:

1) God's Holy Spirit

2) God's Word

3) The souls of human beings.

These are _____ in nature and exist for and in relationship.

These are the _____ of the Kingdom (discipleship) life.

How do we love as God loves us?

_____ – Hebrew expression (Old Testament) of God's Love that includes goodness, kindness, grace, mercy, unending faithfulness (unconditional)

_____ – Greek word (New Testament) for God's unconditional, unfailing, sacrificial, self-giving love

Every other expression of love finds its _____ in God's love (1 John 4:19).

RELATIONSHIPS

Kingdom Currency – Loving Relationships
- Fruit of the Spirit - Galatians 5:22-23
- Personally - Proverbs 31:10-31; I Corinthians 13:4-8a
- In Home - Ephesians 5:21-33
- In Church - Book of I John
- In Community - Matthew 22:37-39; 5:43-44
- Parable of Sower - Matthew 13:3-9; 18-23 (emphasis v. 23)

World's Currency – Stuff/Success
- Satan ("Self") as lord – Lust and selfish desire
- Lusts of the flesh - Galatians 5:16-21
- Parable of Sower - Matthew 13:3-9; 18-23 (emphasis vv. 19-22)
- Selfishness, flesh, and world - Romans 1; Galatians 6:7-9

SEXUALITY

Kingdom Currency - Christ as Lord – Agape
- Marriage as One Woman, One Man - Genesis 2:24; Matthew 19:5-6
- Our bodies as part of Body of Christ, Temple of Holy Spirit - I Corinthians 5:13; 6:19
- Sexual Purity and Blessing - I Corinthians 6:18; Ephesians 5:3

World's Currency – Satan ("Self") as lord – Porneia
- Depravity of man (all sexual sin) - Romans 1 (emphasis v. 24-26)
- Lusts of the flesh - Galatians 5:16-19
- Lust, Sin, Death - James 1:15

Flee 'porneia' (_____). Every sin a man does is outside the body; but the sexually impure sins against his own body. - 1 Corinthians 6:18

There is a difference between a _____ and a struggle. For our purposes…

A stronghold is what one has _____ submitted to and often gives into in one's weakest moments (even while professing to not want to submit to it).

A struggle is something you _____ against because you are aware of it and do not desire to have it in your life. You will overcome if you continue to walk in faith—believe in God's overcoming Truth and act accordingly, even when you do struggle.

> *Hesed/Agape or Porneia/Lust cannot WILLINGLY exist together in your heart. One or the other will win out. Which are you choosing?*

Love and Lust…Pornography and Porneia

Recall "One Couple's Battle with Porn/Porneia" in Chapter 13, p. 65, Print edition.

Porn/Pornography – the enemy's deception in our culture that includes only the active _____ of looking at and engaging in sexual immorality. This can be handled through software "blocks/filters" on digital and other screens.

Porneia – the sexual immorality that remains in our _____ and _____.

> ### Discussion
> How does understanding the difference between porn and porneia help you recognize and deal with these issues in your life, marriage, and relationships?
>
> Discuss as a couple from both sides of the relationship.

Recall "The Cookie Jar" in Chapter 13, p. 66, Print edition.

Small Group Discussion

What comes to mind as you read and think through this satire? What about loving discipline? Entitlement as love? Expectations in love? Other?

How has your understanding and acceptance of this kind of love and discipline impacted your life, love, and relationships?

From the "Who'd You Buy The Roses For?" story in Chapter 13, p. 69, Print edition.

A) What does this story say to you personally?

B) Have you ever been guilty of buying roses (or other gifts) with your focus on what you would receive in return?

C) Have you ever been in a relationship where someone "bought you roses" for themselves? What were those relationships like?

Self and Lust: A Modern-day Movie Biblical Story Mash-up

Recall "The Boat and the Temptation" story about *Fireproof: The Movie* and King David's story of lust and adultery in 2 Samuel 11 (p. 71, Print edition).

What was/is the telling pre-cursor to falling for temptation and into sin?

_____-_____ .

Self-absorbed thinking _____ for the enemy to tempt us.

We then have the choice to avoid the temptation and sin or give into it.

The sooner we _____our thinking, including at the very beginning as we dwell on our self, the easier it is to avoid the temptation.

The more we think about _____ the easier it is to give into the temptation, follow through on the sin, and even cover it up and be blind to it in our own eyes.

That's the _____ of self, lust, pride, and sin.

The sooner we _____ to _____ and live for Christ and His love, the _____we are in Him to overcome any temptation.

Hesed/Agape – The Real Truth About Real Love

God's love is an _____ commitment, a choice, and an act of the will. Love is also an _____ investment in others.

The Full-Orbed Love of God

God's love is a _____-_____ (complete and multi-dimensional) love seen in the stories of two men who approached Christ in Scripture...the leper (Mark 1:40-42) and the rich young ruler (Mark 10:17-22). Christ's love for the leper was expressed in _____ that moved Him to heal the young man. The Greek word, splanchnizomai, means to be moved with compassion or pity.

Food for thought: "Does God/Jesus always love perfectly?"

Christ's love for the rich young ruler was rooted in agapao and expressed in the need for the _____ in his heart to set him free. Agapao deals with love for others that esteems them above self and prefers God above all else.

> ## Discussion
>
> God's love in Christ was displayed perfectly to both men and yet we often struggle with His actions toward the rich young ruler being described in stronger terms of love than what was displayed toward the leper.
>
> How might this help you understand and live out God's love in your life and relationships?

God's Covenant Order

Based on God's Word, what is the order of His Covenant?

What are God's, and therefore should be our, priorities when it comes to relationships?

Priority of Relationships

1) We love because He first loved us – we cannot know love apart from God (1 John 4:19). Love must originate and be found in Him.

   In our love for Him and others we are actually given four commands summed up in the two greatest commands found initially in Deuteronomy 6:4-5 and then repeated in Mark 12:29-31 and Matthew 22:37-39.

2) The First Command, Part 1 - Honor and worship The Lord as One and Only God (Deuteronomy 6:4; Mark 12:29)

3) The First and Greatest command, Part 2 - Love the Lord with all you are (Matthew 22:37-38; Mark 12:30)

4) Living the First Command - Seek The Lord and His Kingdom and righteousness first, above everything else in your life and with all your heart (Jeremiah 29:11-13; Matthew 6:33)

5) The Second Command, Part 1 - Love yourself—the self that God created you to be and recreated you to be in Christ (Matthew 22:39; Mark 12:31; Ephesians 2:10)—so you can die to yourself and fulfill the second command.

Loving my neighbor (all others), continuing with priority and order:

6) Second command, Part 2 - Love your neighbor as you love yourself (Matthew 22:39; Mark 12:31)

   - Marriage – _____ and highest of human relationship; as one in Christ this new "disciple" takes priority over either spouse (Matthew 19:4-6)

   - Spouse – _____ Christ and His Bride (Ephesians 5:21-27; 32-33)

   - Children – God builds His family with Godly _____ (Malachi 2:13-16; Ephesians 6:4)

   - Family members (I Timothy 3:5; 5:4, 8)

   - Friends/Family of God (Galatians 6:10; 1 Peter 2:17); also remember Christ's words regarding family (Luke 8:20-22)

   - Others/Worldly Acquaintances (Romans 12:18, 21; Galatians 6:10)

   - Enemies (Matthew 5:11, 44; Luke 10:30-37; Romans 12:14)

_____ reveal who is Lord/lord in our life.

Priorities also order our _____ - _____ and our relationships.

Love requires _____ ; that is what love does, as we've established in Christ's life and teaching, and in God's Word and commands for us to love as He loved us.

This is how we _____ as His disciples to grow His Church and Kingdom.

Recall "The Rest of the Story" at the end of Chapter 16, p. 81, Print edition.

Small Group Discussion

Take an honest self-assessment and discuss how you're doing when it comes to loving others according the priorities laid out in God's Word and Covenant order.

What are you doing well?

What needs to change?

How will you assure that this change happens for His Kingdom and Glory?

Action Item

Find a small group (or form one) with the focus of growing together in Christ and with others in His Love, holding each other accountable to do so.

> *"To be faithful in every circumstance means that we have only one loyalty, and that is to our Lord... We will be loyal to work, to service, to anything, but do not ask us to be loyal to Jesus Christ... The idea is not that we do work for God, but that we are so loyal to Him that He can do His work through us —"I reckon on you for extreme service, with no complaining on your part and no explanation on Mine." God wants to use us as He used His own Son.*
>
> — Oswald Chambers, *My Utmost for His Highest*

NOTES

MARRIAGE: IN GOD'S IMAGE

Key Concepts

- In God's design, every marriage is a covenant elevating this to the most important of all human relationships.

- Marriage is the union of differences. Communication is at the core of Unity.

- God's design for marriage covenant is a lifetime commitment.

- Two pairs of P.A.N.T.S. essential for Marriage…

    - Proper Authority Needed to Succeed

    - Proper Attitude Needed to Serve

- Marriage always reflects on Christ and His Bride, The Church, and on His Gospel.

- Three Keys to Agape Marriage: 1) Servant's Heart; 2) Humility; 3) Submission.

- Forgiveness is mandatory. Trust is earned. These go together but they are not the same thing.

- Unconditional (Agape) Love = Give 100%; Expect 0%!

- Meeting each other's needs requires daily dying to self through communication and submission in humility, integrity, and purity.

The Highest of Human Relationships

Many would agree that the Bible is "the greatest love letter ever written," we can take it a step further and declare it as the "greatest _____ ever written!" Reasons for this include:

The Creation design itself of _____ and _____;

The image of God reflected in the _____ and the _____;

The concept of Covenant ordained by God through marriage as the relationship that symbolizes His covenant with His people Israel, Christ and His Bride, The Church, and the marriage of one man and one woman in a lifetime commitment.

Every single word in _____ is written to one, two, or all three of the following:

1) God's Covenant with His Bride, Israel;

2) Christ's Covenant with His Bride, The Church;

3) Covenant marriage between one man/one woman.

Are we giving marriage its proper place and honor?

> *Honoring marriage begins long before you say, "I do," and extends throughout marriage and beyond. God's truth about honoring marriage is about honoring His creation in relationships, sexuality, marriage, and family, and that is not for His sake, it is for ours!*

Marriage is the #2 Priority

Refer back to "Priority of Relationships" above.

Marriage is to be esteemed, second only to _____ , above every other institution and relationship in our culture, including The Church, as it preceded and is implicitly and explicitly given such honor in Scripture.

Recall the story in Chapter 17, p. 87, Print edition.

Discussion

What does the story bring to mind and how do you prioritize your marriage?

Do you have a similar story that you can share?

Share how The Spirit is confirming or teaching you with regard to honoring your marriage and spouse?

Marriage Should Be Honored By All

> *"Marriage should be honored by all, and the marriage bed kept pure, for God will judge the adulterer and all the sexually immoral."*
>
> Hebrews 13:4

All means all! Not just those married, remarried, or planning to marry. _____ .

This means that everyone is to honor marriage in his or her _____ and _____ . Simply put, sex is _____ for marriage…period.

Our Creator God began everything in time and history with a relationship of love known as _____ …the closest we can come in human experience to His agape love expressed in covenant commitment.

It's all in line with His sacrificial, selfless kind of love— _____ !

Perfect model for _____ is Christ and His Bride, The Church. (Ephesians 5:21-33)

The goal of every relationship is to _____ Christ.

God has shown us how much He _____ marriage in His design and highest desire for its _____ , His command that all should honor it, and its reflection of His image and our relationship with Him.

Let's connect the dots with regard to His Lordship, our discipleship relationship with Him, and all loving relationships finding their _____ _____ in the marriage relationship.

Three Keys to Building Agape Marriages/Relationships

Recognizing God's Love and Authority as the Foundation for all other relationships:

His Covenant Order in relationships exists because…No matter how desperately we try we cannot love others until we have learned to love ourselves. And we cannot love ourselves until we first love God with all we are (Mark 12:29-31). This allows Him to show us who we are recreated to be in Christ (Ephesians 2:10). We love because He first loved us (1 John 4:19).

Following are the 3 Keys to Agape Marriage/Relationships:

1) Love God with all you are! (Deuteronomy 6:4-6; Mark 12:29-20) –
   _____ is the key found in what we are called to do in honoring one
   another in relationships and particularly in marriage (Ephesians 5:21-28). Husbands,
   in particular, as servant-leaders, are to lay down our life for our wife (Philippians
   2:5-8). This is Christ's example to His Bride, The Church.

2) Love Who You Are in Christ! (Matthew 22:39: Mark 12:31) – The second key is:
   _____ as confidence and contentment in who we are so we can place others
   above self (Philippians 2:3-8; John 13:3; Romans 12:3). Husbands, we must lay down
   our lifestyles and place the needs and desires of our wife above our own. Had Jesus
   not surrendered His lifestyle in heaven first, then He could not have become fully
   God and fully man and His death on The Cross (what we always equate with "giving
   up our life for our wife") would have meant nothing.

3) Love Others As You Love Yourself! (Matthew 22:39; Mark 12:31) Are you beginning
   to see God's design for loving marriages/relationships? The third key: _____
   as seen in Jesus washing His disciples' feet (John 13:1-5, 12-17). Here we see the
   coming together of love (v.1), humility (v.3), serving (vv.4-5), authority (v.13),
   and now discipleship (vv.14-17).

   _____ marriages and relationships are built on these three keys as Agape!

Imagine once again what our marriages, families, and churches would look like if we made disciples that loved God with all we are and above everything else, and from there, loved who we are in Christ so we could love one another as Christ loved us. Our marriage and family should be integral as His Church, not just go to Church!

This is Christ in us and through us,
as we love others in His Covenant Order:
Marriage ➡ *Spouse* ➡ *Children*
and Family ➡ *His Church* ➡ *The World*

"Christ's idea is that we serve Him by being the servants of other men...He says that in His Kingdom he that is greatest shall be the servant of all. The real test of the saint is not preaching the gospel, but washing disciples' feet, that is, doing the things that do not count in the actual estimate of men but count everything in the estimate of God."

— Oswald Chambers, *My Utmost for His Highest*

Recall story of Ami's call and request in Chapter 18, p. 95, Print edition.

Discussion

What areas in your marriage and with your spouse have caused the greatest conflict?

How might the 3 Keys to Agape Marriage help resolve the conflict?

What do you need to do in your role and response to love as Christ loves us?

Q&A

A) What is your "clothes basket" that you fully expect your spouse to do with no help on your part?

B) How does your spouse feel about it?

C) Is there an agreement that some issues and responsibilities are yours and some are your spouse's?

D) If not, what can you do to step up and serve your marriage and spouse?

Biblical Tips for Navigating Marriage

Authority in Marriage

P.A.N.T.S.

Who wears them in your Marriage?

Pair #1 - P_____ A_____ N_____ To S_____

and

Pair #2 - P_____ A_____ N_____ To S_____

We all love to wear Pair #1, but according to God's Word there is no Pair #1 unless we are willing to wear Pair #2!

Recall "The Clothes Basket on the Stairs" Parody.

Forgiveness and Trust

In almost every case with struggling couples, no matter what the symptoms are, there are major foundational issues rooted in unforgiveness and distrust. While these are related they are not the same thing.

Forgiveness is _____ (Matthew 6:14-15; Ephesians 4:32).

Trust is _____ (John 2:24).

Forgiveness is a command to be obeyed, not feelings to be processed contrary to modern day thinking and counseling. There are emotions to be processed, but whether or not we are obedient determines who is guiding the processing of our related emotions. Obedience gives way to The Holy Spirit; disobedience and harboring unforgiveness to the enemy. Your choice. But it will have a tremendous impact on your ability to rebuild trust!

Obedience ties _____ to God's Truth. Disobedience ties it to our _____ .

How might this Biblical understanding help you to resolve issues and build/rebuild trust in your relationship?

Action Items

- Today, take time to write down any bitterness or unforgiveness that you've held on to.
- Write down issue(s) and names. Begin with your spouse.
- Pray and ask God to forgive you for your disobedience.
- Then ask Him to give you the strength to specifically forgive each person and situation.

Unconditional Love and Marriage

Simple Biblical definition for Love based on The Cross: Give _____%; Expect _____%!

Expectations and _____ will naturally occur in our flesh. The issue is how you respond and how you define your spouse, yourself, and your relationship when they are not met. Do you play God or do you leave that up to Him?

Learn to _____ and _____ even when expectations are not met. More of them will be realized over time and you will become the person who is more interested in looking to meet your spouse's needs rather than always expecting that yours be met.

> ## Discussion
>
> How does this impact your thinking regarding marriage, divorce, remarriage, and adultery?
>
> Does this represent a truth and grace interpretation?
>
> If so, how does it help you in your situation or with others who may have experienced divorce and remarriage?
>
> If not, how does your interpretation align with other truths in Scripture regarding relationships, sexuality, marriage, divorce, and porneia/adultery?

God's Word on Marriage, Adultery, Divorce and Remarriage

1) God ordained Marriage to reflect His Image and to be in lifetime covenant
   - Genesis 2:24; Matthew 19:5-6

2) Marriage - symbolic of God and Israel; and Christ and His Bride, the Church
   - Jeremiah 31:31-32; Ephesians 5:25-27

3) God hates divorce and the breaking of the covenant - Malachi 2:16

4) There are many reasons Moses allowed for divorce, all found in the "hardness of our hearts," and marriage requires serious forethought and consideration before entering into it - Matthew 19:7-10

5) There is NO Scriptural basis for remarriage after divorce (with two concerns subject to Scriptural interpretation)
   - ∞ Marital unfaithfulness/sexual infidelity - Matthew 19:9;
   - ∞ Unbelieving spouse leaves the marriage - 1 Corinthians 7:10-16

6) One allowance for remarriage (Death of spouse - 1 Corinthians 7:39) as all other remarriage, even in two reasons directly above, still ends in adultery for both spouses upon remarriage - Mark 10:11; Luke 16:18

7) Divorce and remarriage - not the unpardonable sin (Blasphemy or rejection of Holy Spirit received only through Christ) - Matthew 12:31

Recall story of Marriage and Family Conference in Cameroon Chapter 20, pp. 103-105, Print edition.

Marriage Activity – *this will bless your marriage (do it at least once annually)*

Willard Harley in his book, *His Needs, Her Needs,* lists the top 10 needs, by gender, in Marriage based on 30,000 couples over 25 years.

Women	Men
1) Affection (read Love)	1) Sexual Fulfillment (read Sex)
2) Conversation	2) Recreational Companionship
3) Honesty and Openness	3) Attractive Spouse
4) Financial Support	4) Domestic Support
5) Family Commitment	5) Admiration (read Respect)

Dr. Harley's list gives you an idea. Your list may be similar or quite different but in my experience the lists are usually comparable to his. Here's the activity…

1. Individually rank and personally define your needs.
2. List ways your spouse can meet each need as you define it.

Share and communicate with your submissive spouse how you defined your needs and how they can be met. Whatever you do be sure to keep in mind that these are done in mutual Love and Respect for each other and agreement is mandatory in all of this.

NOTES

MARRIAGE, FAMILY, AND PARENTING GOD'S WAY

Key Concepts

- In God's design, every family starts with marriage: one man/one woman for life.

- Families are the "building blocks" of Christ's Family, The Church.

- Developing character or the heart of Christ should be the first priority in parenting—discipling them in the nurture and admonition of the Lord!

- Children are a gift from The Lord, the greatest blessing/burden rolled into one.

- Parenting is the first and most powerful depiction of Godly Love and Authority (good or bad) in a child's life.

- Parenting moves children from respect for parental authority to self-control and respect for God's Authority in Christ.

- Parenting is to reflect the Love and Authority of God according to His Truth revealed in His Son, His Word, and His Spirit.

- Parenting and family are to reflect the image of God through His Truth and Love.

- Parenting includes loving discipline and punishment, ultimately discipling our children in Christ.

- Discipline includes the foundations, guidelines and boundaries, in line with God's Word/Truth, in which we can most fully and freely mature and grow.

- Punishment is the loving, corrective response to our children when they step outside the established disciplines in line with God's Word.

- Punishment should never be done in pride or anger but in humility to disciple our child's heart rather than simply change behavior.

- Three D's to consider in loving punishment: 1) Danger; 2) Disrespect; 3) Defiance.

Read the quotes throughout this section and recall the two contrasting stories of home at the beginning of Chapter 21, p. 111, Print edition. Take time to discuss the following:

How have you approached marriage and family in your home?

On a scale of 1-10 (with 10 being highest) what priority have you placed on your marriage? Your family?

What score would your spouse give you? Your children?

What score would you give your spouse?

A child's first, and likely most lasting, concept of God, good or bad, centers on what they see in their earthly _____ and particularly in their father.

God, The Author, gives the responsibility of being the loving authority in every child's life to _____ .

> *"In God's design and mandate, discipleship is to begin in the home and the church benefits and is stronger when this happens. When it's not happening, there's not enough 'church' to overcome what is lacking in the home."*
>
> — Greg Williams

God's Design for Parenting and Family

1) Parents are the _____ *and* _____ *disciplers/educators* of their children. Deuteronomy 6:1-9 (signifies utmost importance in passing on education to our children)

Parents, we are to take the first and highest responsibility for training up our children—not the school and their teachers, not the government, not coaches, and not even pastors or ministers.

2) Discipling and educating our children requires time and effort to know and train them. Proverbs 22:6, *Train up a child in the way he should go, even when he is old he will not depart from it.* Ephesians 6:4, *Fathers, do not provoke your children to anger, but bring them up in the discipline and instruction of the Lord.*

Ancient Proverb – **"Bend a tree when it's young."**

Biblical parenting requires time, _____ , investment, and effort!

One of the greatest lies from the pits of hell... *"Quality time equals quantity time."*

> *"Children are the greatest blessing and greatest burden all rolled into one."*
>
> — Monte Wilkinson, Lead Minister,
> Northeast Christian Church, Lexington, KY

God's Word declares that children are a reward or heritage from The Lord (Psalm 127). If we only see the burden, then we miss the joys of His blessing to us.

Scripture also declares that there is a burden in the responsibility of training them up in The Lord (Proverbs 22:6; Ephesians 6:4). If we only look for blessings, then we miss the lessons and needed pruning in our lives and in our children's as well.

Recall "The Church Prioritized" and "The Church Comes First" stories in Chapter 22, p. 117, Print edition.

Q&A

A) In what ways have you prioritized church, work, or other things over your family?

B) How has this impacted your family and your relationship with your spouse and children?

C) What do you desire for your family with regard to faith, love, and relationships?

D) What changes need to be made to prioritize your marriage and family in line with God's Covenant order so they know of their importance and value to you?

E) How does this ultimately point them to God as a loving and holy Dad?

The Importance of Character in Life…Character in Scripture

Character brings about God's _____ – The Prayer of Jabez (1 Chronicles 4:9-10).

Character stimulates a desire for and willingness to seek out and understand Truth (Acts 17:11).

Abraham Lincoln, paraphrasing Proverbs 22:6, said, "There is just one way to bring up a child in the way he should go, and that is to travel that way yourself."

Character in Parenting – Building Our Children's Self-Worth

Good parents desire God's blessings in their _____ lives as well as for them to seek after and understand God's Truth.

The best way to encourage character, integrity, and Truth in our children's lives is to model them in our own _____ .

One of the enemy's greatest tricks, common to all of us, is to focus and reward one another based on _____ or _____ . While we need to be encouraged when we have done what is right or good, God knows that the true development happens in our heart in the formation of character.

The world is mesmerized by self-esteem, but in reality that is just another prideful motive that ultimately destroys. The real trophy, or jewel, that our children need is to know their

_____ .

Self-discipline ➡ self-control ➡ self-respect ➡ self-worth ➡ self-love

This aligns with the greatest commands in that it takes self-discipline/self-control to die to self and worship and love God above all.

Maturity in faith and worship produces the self-respect that comes from knowing and loving who we are in Him, which gives us our self-worth, enabling us to truly love others.

> *"Happy will that house be in which relations are formed from character."*
> — Ralph Waldo Emerson

Praise – Two Kinds

1) For _____   **2) For** _____

Fill in the columns…How do you encourage your children for accomplishments or performance? How do you encourage character? Which do you focus on the most?

> *"What can you do to promote world peace?*
> *Go home and love your family."*
> — Mother Teresa

Character, Integrity, and Legacy

Whatever you invest into your children will become the _____ that you leave.

Research shows over and over again that despite the Internet, media, peers, and other influencers, _____ still have by far the greatest influence on their children.

"What _____ will your influence leave?"

Will it be one of _____ for Christ or will it be for the world?

The second greatest influence is their _____ . How are you guiding and helping to shape their faith? They will stand or fall based on how you _____ and instill that faith in them.

> *"Every family is a little church."*
> — Dennis Rainey, Founder, FamilyLife

Biblical Discipleship in Parenting

Parenting is ultimately about _____ your children to know Christ as their Savior and Lord and to grow in Him.

Biblical _____ is actually the boundaries, guidelines, and foundations found in God's Word - Absolute Truth on which you establish or build your marriage, family, parenting (all relationships).

Biblical _____ is actually what occurs when children fail to stay 'inside' or intentionally move 'outside' the disciplines that have been established in order to guide someone back within those truths in which they can most fully and freely grow – Deuteronomy 6:4-9; Proverbs 22:6; Ephesians 6:1-4; Hebrews 12:1-15.

Keys to Biblical (Loving and Healthy) Discipline and Punishment:

The following is to help you establish disciplines and guidelines and administer loving punishment as needed according to God's Word and our Heavenly Father's example found in Hebrews 12:1-15.

1) Discipline and punishment are both part of God's _____ and _____ toward us - His Word must be the source in establishing discipline and administering punishment.

2) Discipline is _____ first in our lives before applied in others – lessons are caught more than taught.

3) Be clear and consistent - both discipline and punishment must be _____ communicated and _____ applied in your life and in parenting.

4) Three _____ for punishment:

   A) Disrespect – ignorant or initial willfulness

   B) Defiance – clear, continued disrespect toward your authority

   C) Danger – to avoid harm and teach lessons that protect from danger

5) Never punish in _____ or from _____ – be sure to check your own motives and selfishness whenever applying punishment with your children – very difficult in tense and embarrassing moments, but must apply in Love.

6) Punishment and _____ – Punishment fits the crime; give opportunities to reward for good behavior and heart as well as for good response to punishment (train the heart).

7) _____ your children – allow them to be a part of establishing foundations and guidelines based on God's Word as you craft and communicate discipline and punishment. Allow them to define their own punishment to the extent they understand the heart issues and can apply it justly. You keep _____ !

> *"God is willing to place the electric fence before the 1,000 foot cliff. The shock may hurt but you have the chance to learn from it rather than walk off the cliff."*

God's punishment is part of His Love (Hebrews 12:1-15)...very difficult concept in our culture and time. As we apply discipline and punishment with our children in light of His Love, it not only changes our approach it produces better outcomes!

As they have faced their own consequences and His loving, yet tough, punishment we have seen that prayer come to pass and are so excited about how He has drawn them to Him and grown them in Him!

Encouragement & Hope

As Ami and I were raising our children, our prayer and desire was for them to know all of God's love, knowing that every bit of it, even the tough and sometimes painful part, was for their good. Knowing that as His child, they would at some point receive His punishment out of His love, but instead of them running from it and rebelling against Him, we wanted them to see His love and run toward Him.

3 Opportunities for Parents to Disciple/Teach Children – Deuteronomy 6:4-9

1) "Family _____" - meals together, devotionals, family worship, other – all of these offer excellent times for stories, family history, recaps of the day, and provide great chances to go deeper in laughter, tears, and emotion, and especially in teaching and building character and relationships.

2) "Along the _____" - school/team trips, road trips, vacations, drive time, appointments, other – more opportunities to focus the conversation through updates on school events, friends, teams, etc., and include character and relationship development.

3) "_____" - special times and events, Rites of Passage, Passing on a Blessing, others – Focus on God's design and order, including Jewish culture of Biblical times and young adulthood at 13 years of age for boys (bar mitzvah) and 12 years of age for girls (bat mitzvah), respectively, with mature adulthood at 30 years of age (Jesus even honoring this in Public Ministry – Sermon on Mt. at age 30)

   A) Rites of Passage - Family Crest or Symbol captured and given in some way to children along with family/friends' letters of encouragement/ challenge for each child at young adulthood

   B) Ongoing discussions at age-appropriate times (beginning by age 3 with respect for body parts, etc.) about bodies, sexuality, and relationships

Our Family Story: Discipling Our Children

Recall Chapter 25, p. 127, Print edition, about how The Lord led us in raising our children (imperfect but in God's Covenant design). How are we to build the loving fellowship of believers called out as His Church except that we first, just as He did, begin with the loving relationships of marriage and family? This is where both love and leadership are trained and matured in God's design and according to His Word.

Discussion

Talk about what you have done or are doing in your family and parenting that are helping to instill faith, character, and integrity in your children.

What are some things you can add to this list for your children/family?

What might you do differently as a result of going through this series?

Read "Best Decisions I've Made as a Father"…

Fathers…what decisions have you made in your life and how have they impacted your marriage, spouse, and children?

Share some of the decisions that have been a blessing to your spouse and children.

What needs to change, if anything, for you to be intentional about leaving a Godly legacy for your children and family?

NOTES

THE HOME AND RELATIONAL SERVANT-LEADERSHIP IN CHRIST'S FAMILY

> *"Strength of character may be acquired at work, but beauty of character is learned at home. There the affections are trained. There the gentle life reaches us, the true heaven life. In one word, the family circle is the supreme conductor of Christianity."*
>
> — Henry Drummond

Our Family and Christ's Family

The nuclear and extended family and His Family, known as Christ's Church, are inseparable in God's Covenant order and design.

Recall: Galatians 6:10; Ephesians 2:19-22; 1 Timothy 3:1-15, and 1 Peter 4:17 all point to God's design and purpose in creating us in His image, lived out in loving relationships in our families and in His family, Christ's Church.

The enemy battles fervently to _____ marriages and families.

We must _____ our families in helping to build Godly relationships that strengthen His Family, the Church.

Home is where we learn to love, lead, and disciple, and the _____ benefits from focusing on and helping husbands and wives, mothers and fathers, to do so.

Two Stories of Modern-day Home and Church Leadership

Much of the culture of the modern-day Western church has opted for a _____ success model based on marketing principles and attraction rather than a Kingdom fruit model based on disciples maturing and making disciples as branches in The Vine (John 15:1-8).

The currency of Christ's Kingdom is loving relationships and the fruit is disciples making disciples, not just in numbers but in obedience and accountability to His Word and Spirit.

Recall "A Leader in Business and Church…but not at Home" and "Having an Affair with Christ's Bride" in Chapter 26, p. 139, Print edition.

Discussion

Have you seen this in your church or with friends?

How closely do these lifestyle choices hit home with you?

How would your spouse respond to that last question about him/herself?

About you?

As applicable, what will you do differently to change and/or battle against any or all "intruders" on the priorities of your marriage, your spouse, and family?

Loving and Leading in The Home and in His Church

> *The church in America has become so culturally relevant that it has become culturally irrelevant.*

The modern-day American church is so concerned with reaching the culture that we have _____ on numerous issues to the point that we look much like it.

I have given them Your word; and the world has hated them, because they are not of the world, even as I am not of the world. - John 17:14

We want so much to be liked and for His message to be well _____ , we do nearly whatever we can to get the culture to like and accept it. That's not how Jesus described the world responding to Him or His Word.

May God forgive us as we_____ and seek His face to follow His commands for _____ His Church.

Seven general qualifications outlined in 1 Timothy 3:1-7 and Titus 1:5-9:

1) Must be the husband of one wife.

2) He should necessarily be an older person as the Greek word for elder, presbyteros, (Titus 1:5) literally means an older person or advanced in years (relative to eras and lifespans but tied to discipling/guiding one's marriage, family).

3) Ability to teach and lead or shepherd.

4) Personal maturity and behavior.

5) Spiritual maturity in the faith.

6) Good testimony of character in the community.

7) Must be able to relationally servant-lead his family.

Recall "**my personal experience**" in Chapter 27, p. 143, Print edition.

> *We have mastered the art of loving and leading "from afar" in community and systems, such as corporate or governing relationships, all the while neglecting to be obedient to God's Word to love and lead first in the most intimate of relationships—marriage and family!*

_____

_____

_____

_____

_____

_____

_____

The Marriage ➡ Family ➡ Church Leadership Connection

God's Word elevates marriage and family to the unique position of the _____ ground for love and leadership in The Church.

The training ground of marriage and family teaches love, humility, and relational _____-_____ —all required to build Christ's Church on the apostle's teachings and on Him as the Cornerstone. (Ephesians 2:19-22)

Discipleship in the training ground of marriage and family develops love and relational servant-leadership for The Church:

1) Obedience to Christ's model of leadership as submissive, humble service that leads to an _____ of influence – True Authority is the same from the family to the Church to the workplace or culture.

2) Relational servant-leadership is _____ through the most important and intimate of relationships, that of marriage and family.

3) God's Word places a _____ on managing (serving) those in the family/home.

4) Relational servant-leadership is a key factor, along with spiritual maturity, age, experience, teaching, and serving others in the church and community, in developing _____-_____ (Elders and Deacons) in Christ's Church.

Deception and Its Fruit

We must apply God's Word to our lives, homes, and to Christ's Church or we will continue to prioritize cultural success above Kingdom fruit!

We have mastered the art of loving and leading "from afar" in community and systems, such as corporate or governing relationships, all the while neglecting to be obedient to God's Word to love and lead first in the most intimate of relationships—marriage and family!

> *"Do what you will," he warns, "there is going to be some benevolence, as well as some malice, in your patient's soul. The great thing is to direct the malice to his immediate neighbours whom he meets every day and thrust his benevolence out to the remote circumference, to people he does not know. The malice thus becomes wholly real and the benevolence largely imaginary."*
>
> — C. S. Lewis, *The Screwtape Letters*

Humility is key as we determine whether and where we are compromising on God's Word and in His Church:

1) PRIDE – God's Word requires us to first do the work of _____ (raising and training our children as a prerequisite to leading His Church.

2) FEAR – There is a lack of _____ teaching on relationships, sexuality, marriage, and family and relational servant-leadership. We must encourage and hold parents accountable to teach and obey His word on relationships, sexuality, and marriage.

3) DECEPTION – Marriage/Family, relationship and sexuality is _____ by culture and not truthfully defended by our churches as defined in Scripture – we must counter the lies of the world's values on these issues. We must also gently point to freedom and forgiveness found only in Christ and lived out by His grace in our loving obedience to His Word.

4) CONFORMITY – Church leadership decisions conform to the world. We must return to the priorities found in God's Word of _____ relationships over budgets and buildings.

God's design and order for discipleship training in relationships in families _____ both our families and our churches.

Experience and humility gained from relational servant leading in the family_____ both the home and the church.

The wisdom gained from building intimate relationships in the home and holding each other accountable in those relationships produces _____ leadership in church.

A key question for real leadership: "Are you serving your marriage, spouse, and family with as much or more time and effort as you are serving those in the church or those the church calls you to serve?"

Food for thought: Questions to highlight God's design for love and leadership:

1) Do you desire to lead in God's Kingdom?

2) From where will He draw and designate His Kingdom leaders?

3) From where does His Word say the leaders in His Church are to come?

4) Are you preparing yourself to be a leader in His Church, according to His Word, in your marriage and family?

Scriptural and Practical Solutions

Seven solutions from the principles of His Love & Lordship in this book:

As families and The Church focus on the following in obedience-based discipleship, they will become more prevalent in our lives, homes, relationships, and in His Body:

1) The _____ of Christ (Truth) will be evident as our top priority in our lives — Matthew 20:24–28; John 13:1-17.

2) _____ is our response to His Lordship and how we mature in Him — Ephesians 4:13; Hebrews 5:14; James 1:2-4. We will teach disciples how to first understand God's love for us, followed by loving Him with all we are and then loving who we are in Christ so we can love all others—Matthew 22:37-39; Mark 12:29-31. In doing so we will bear fruit and grow in the knowledge of God—Colossians 9:1-11; Galatians 5:22-24.

3) _____ discipleship and maturity in Christ will be the priority and evident in Church teaching and in our relationships and service, beginning in the home and family. We do this by _____ our relationships in His Covenant Order: Christ ➡ Marriage/Family ➡ Church ➡ World. (Genesis 2:24; Matthew 5:19; Hebrews 13:4; Proverbs 22:6; Ephesians 6:1-4)

4) We mature in discipleship and mentoring, and in relationship with Him and others through studying and serving according to His Word–2 Timothy 2:15; Matthew 28:18-20; Hebrews 5:11–6:6. In doing so, we revalue _____ , marriage and family culture that emphasizes:

   - Teaching and accountability in agape relationships and purity in sexuality;

   - Relational servant-leadership modeled and taught in the home;

   - Generational discipleship beginning in the home and reinforced in churches.

5) Maturation in Christ builds a _____ or family-based body of believers rather than corporate and business-based – Ephesians 2:11-22; Ephesians 4. Building _____ is taught as Spiritual Disciplines and Discipleship rather than deferring to the culture's concept of relationships occurring naturally.

6) We live in His _____ priorities according to His Word, which are familial and relational, rooted in character above performance, growth, financial, and numbers served; prioritize family and relationships in selecting leaders and in decision-making – 1 Timothy 3:1-13; Titus 1:6-10

   Our maturity in Christ focuses on and builds a _____ - _____ Church rather than a corporate and business-based model driven by goals and outcomes.

   The Biblical emphasis of _____ and loving relationships as Kingdom fruit takes priority and drives decision-making with regard to growth, finances, service, programs and all other elements rather than the reverse.

7) Walking in His Covenant order, we build an Acts 2 familial Church that makes and matures disciples who serve, give, and share as a result of His priority principles – Acts 2; Matthew 7:21-23

   A _____ and _____ Church develops disciples who serve, give, share, and lead as a result of priority principles of Christ's Lordship and our discipleship.

"What Would Jesus Say to Today's Megachurch?"

Recall the story from Chapter 29, p. 151, Print edition, and the "Reveal" survey.

Discussion

What does the conversation regarding Jesus' response to today's megachurches say with regard to our approach to churches and discipleship?

Does your church have a similar grouping of attendees as those in the Reveal survey? Which group would you fit into?

What do those outcomes suggest about discipleship in today's churches?

What are the priorities in your church on Lordship, discipleship, marriage/family, and servant-leadership?

NOTES

WISE AS SERPENTS, GENTLE AS DOVES

Key Concepts

- We must be prepared as Christ's disciples to take His message to the world.

- Preparation calls for us to be studied, obedient, wise, and gracious.

- Modern-day outcomes include emotionally based "salvation," a lack of obedience-based discipleship, spiritual immaturity, and fleshly driven service.

- Cultural Christianity places emphasis on people above God.

- Restoring the foundations of Lordship, discipleship, Godly marriage, families, and relationships is essential to reviving The Church.

- The greatest destroyer of loving relationships is sexual immorality or porneia.

- The culture spreads the "safe sex" message of porneia as perfectly fine and disguised as "education."

- The fruit of the sexual revolution in our families, churches, and culture is immorality and destruction as we are reaping what we have sown.

- The churches' responses is predominantly symptomatic.

- The Church needs to respond with the foundational principles of relational integrity, sexual purity within marriages, and families at the center with churches and families then supporting each other in obedience-based discipleship.

- God's order is to move from the individual to relationships to community to corporate or systemic. If we do not heed His Word with individuals and in relationships, we will not be able to curtail it in our communities or systems.

- The Scriptural paradigm of the Love and Lordship message is:
  Lordship ➡ Discipleship ➡ Relationship ➡ Sin/Issues/Problems

> *"We are apt to forget that a man is not only committed to Jesus Christ for salvation; he is committed to Jesus Christ's view of God, of the world, of sin and of the devil, and this will mean that he must recognize the responsibility of being transformed by the renewing of his mind."*
>
> — Oswald Chambers, *My Utmost for His Highest*

I highly recommend you read *Theology of the Body* by Christopher West, as it is an excellent and powerful rendering of God's design for relationship, marriage, sexuality, and family as foundational to His Creative Order and Covenant relationships in His image.

> *"Christ's mission is to restore the order of love in a world seriously distorted by sin. And the union of the sexes, as always, lies at the basis of the human "order of love." (This is) obviously "important with regard to marriage." However it is equally essential and valid for the (understanding) of man in general: for the fundamental problem of understanding him and for the self-understanding of his being in the world."*
>
> — Christopher West, *Theology of the Body*

In order to take His Gospel message to a lost and dying world, we, as Christ followers, must recapture this Biblical thinking of the spiritual and physical together in whom we are created to be, and recreated to be, in Christ!

"Created in His image," "male and female He created them," "the two shall become one flesh," and "The Word became flesh" are all central to God's design and His Gospel message that we must share in how we live and relate in honoring our spirit and body, along with His message that "marriage should be honored by all" (Hebrews 13:4).

Only as we bring all of His Truth together in word and deeds can we reach a world enslaved to the enemy's lies to destroy all of God's design and order and Christ's restoration and redemption of all of Creation.

Serpents and Doves...Taking His Message to The World

Jesus spent two of the three years of His public ministry _____ His disciples before sending them out with this warning, Matthew 10:16, ***Behold, I send you out as sheep in the midst of wolves. Therefore be wise as serpents and harmless as doves.***

The culture, through our _____ and government, has co-opted the Gospel message for some time, couching it in familiar terms but exporting death and destruction. Abortion couched in _____ rights language, contraception in terms of health and _____ - _____ , and _____ labeled as free speech.

The _____ has done little in many cases to counter the messages and efforts, and in other cases has helped to spread the demoralizing and devastating outcomes.

When we comply, by _____ or _____ , we are allowing the enemy to attack the very foundations of God's creation and order from the beginning.

As stated earlier in this book, _____ / _____ is the greatest destroyer of love and relationship and the only thing that will overcome it is the power of the Gospel lived out through His families and Church.

The Church must not be afraid to _____ His whole Truth regarding relationships, marriage, family, and sexuality.

Exporting Porn and "Churchianity"

Recall the story of Pastor Shu, Chapter 29, p. 162, Print edition.

Discussion

What did this story reveal about how our churches in western culture are responding to the crisis of porneia (sexual immorality) in our relationships, marriages, and families?

What has been your experience when it comes to these issues in our schools, government, and media?

What has the response been in your family? In your church?

What do we need to do differently?

Look at the root of the sin and porneia that the enemy uses to destroy lives, relationships, and communities through divorce and broken families.

The result is that we hinder our ability to serve the Church, and ultimately cripple its ministry. Most of it is exported from a pornified culture rooted in _____ !

> *"It would seem that Our Lord finds our desires not too strong, but too weak. We are half-hearted creatures, fooling about with drink and sex and ambition when infinite joy is offered us, like an ignorant child who wants to go on making mud pies in a slum because he cannot imagine what is meant by the offer of a holiday at the sea. We are far too easily pleased."*
> — Oswald Chambers, *The Weight of Glory*

Current Outcomes/Potential Struggles – Present and Eternal

Issues that we need to address in order to come against what the world and enemy of our souls are pandering, and then _____, yet graciously, step up and proclaim God's Truth.

- _____-driven salvation
- Very lacking in _____-based discipleship
- Spiritually _____, fleshly driven service
- Focus on _____ above God
- Churches and Christians that look and act like the _____ – Conformed to the world

Jesus' prophetic warning to these issues is found in Matthew 7:21-23...

Not everyone who says to Me, 'Lord, Lord,' will enter the kingdom of heaven, but he who does the will of My Father who is in heaven will enter. Many will say to Me on that day, 'Lord, Lord, did we not prophesy in Your name, and in Your name cast out demons, and in Your name perform many miracles?' And then I will declare to them, 'I never knew you; DEPART FROM ME, YOU WHO PRACTICE LAWLESSNESS.'

> *When the foundations are destroyed, what can the righteous do?* - Psalm 11:3

Who's Discipling Our Youth?

Whoever is _____ our children up in the way they want them to go will have their hearts and minds.

We are called to do this as Christian _____ , first and foremost, and then with Godly ministers, teachers, and servant-leaders to reinforce.

We are _____ to be diligent in training up our children in what we provide for them and what we protect them from. – Deuteronomy 6:4-9; Proverbs 22:6; Ephesians 6:4

Following are the 3 diagrams from the book that illustrate the current paradigm; the church's current symptomatic responses and; a proposed response based on God's Covenant Design. The purpose is to give us a look at these and through discussion and prayer formulate a response that will help us battle that culture and restore integrity in relationships and purity in sexuality expressed in marriage, family, and Christ's Church to positively impact our culture and world.

The Current Paradigm

FRUIT OF THE CURRENT PARADIGM–
CONFORMED TO THE WORLD–REAPING WHAT
WE'VE SOWN

Fruits

Divorce   Divorce

Teen/Unwed Pregnancies   Depression

Suicidal Tendencies   Abortion

Addiction   Cohabitation

Promiscuity STDs   Pornography

Roots/Foundation
Planned Parenthood/SIECUS/AFY–Condom Promotion,
Free Sex Education 70%+ Of Today's Youth

Galatians 6:7-8, *Do not be deceived, God is not mocked; for whatever a man sows, this he will also reap. For the one who sows to his own flesh will from the flesh reap corruption, but the one who sows to the Spirit will from the Spirit reap eternal life.*

The _____ and _____ remain the same in this current paradigm with several hours weekly or even daily in schools that are exponentially multiplied as they direct youth and children to their Internet and media presence.

Contrast that with how churches _____ to _____ the message with symptomatic programs that may add up to a few hours annually in youth groups and sermons.

Knowledge-based _____ , evident in the programs and outcomes currently, is not discipleship. Unless we change the paradigm to _____-_____ discipleship in loving relationships we will continue to win a few hearts while losing many more.

In our desire to see people saved, we've " _____ " His order to draw people in to hear the Gospel message, which is so important.

The _____ has taken full advantage of our heartfelt but misplaced priorities when it comes to expecting obedience (John 14:15, 21; 1 Peter 1:22; 1 John 2:5; 5:2).

There's a better way! Obedience-based discipleship under Christ's teaching in our families with churches stepping up to reinforce the messages and help encourage obedience and accountability with grace and Truth!

Strengthen _____ and _____ and we all win!

Word of Hope - "Do I believe that God can deal with my 'yesterday,' and make it as though it had never been? I either do not believe he can, or I do not want Him to. Forgiveness, which is so easy for us to accept, cost God the agony of Calvary. When Jesus Christ says, 'Sin no more,' He conveys the power that enables a man not to sin any more, and that power comes by right of what He did on the Cross." Oswald Chambers, *Still Higher for His Highest*

Current Church Paradigm: Conformed to the World/Reaping What Is Sown

In being conformed to the world, we are _____ exactly what we've sown!

Make a tree good and its fruit will be good, or make a tree bad and its fruit will be bad, for a tree is recognized by its fruit. — Matthew 12:33

The modern church has primarily implemented symptomatic strategies and programs captured in the following graphic:

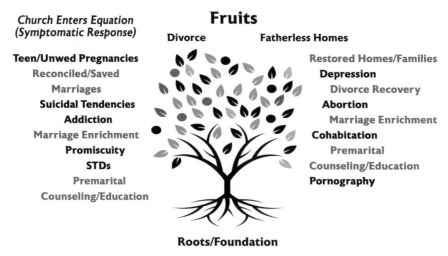

FRUIT OF THE CURRENT PARADIGM –
CONFORMED TO THE WORLD-REAPING WHAT
WE'VE SOWN

Romans 12:2, *And do not be conformed to this world, but be transformed by the renewing of your mind, so that you may prove what the will of God is, that which is good and acceptable and perfect.*

A symptomatic response does not deal with the seeds that are sown but simply attempts to "paint the fruit" and make it appear better.

The "New" Old Paradigm – His Loving Discipleship in Relationships

Check out this visual of what this "new" paradigm may look like in line with obedience-based discipleship in our homes and churches...

"CUNNING AS SERPENTS, GENTLE AS DOVES"

Fruits

Healthy Marriages	**Healthy Families**
Divorce	Fatherless Homes
Teen/Unwed Pregnancies	**Vibrant Churches**
Reconciled/Saved Marriages	Depression
Suicidal Tendencies	Abortion
Divorce Recovery	**Restored Homes/Families**
Addiction	Cohabitation
Marriage Enrichment	**Addiction Recovery**
Promiscuity STDs	Pornography
Premarital Counseling/Education	**Marriage Mentoring**

The Church in partnership with marriages/families to work at the root cause and lay a firm foundation and future success.

Roots/Foundation
Marriage and Family/Discipleship
Truth Foundation in Homes

God's _____ and _____ for obedience-based discipleship is the key.

In His design, discipleship is lived out in loving and respectful _____ built on the Love and Lordship we have in Christ.

Discussion

How can we build loving relationships in our homes that help overcome the world's teachings?

What might it look like for our churches to support (not just teach about) these kind of relationships?

How could this encourage stronger discipleship based on obedience?

What difference might this make in developing disciples and relational servant-leaders in our families? In our churches?

What is the potential impact of these relationships, discipleship, and servant-leaders in our culture?

Changing the Paradigm: Transformed by Renewing our Minds

Changing our culture begins with our own changed lives by the _____ and salvation of Christ.

This is done through obedience-based discipleship under Christ's _____ .

He takes _____ over every aspect of our lives.

In order to gain our lives we must _____ them to Him (Luke 9:24).

Why Love & Lordship
Authority (The Author's Design)

Lordship (Authority)

⬇

Discipleship

⬇

Relationship

⬇

Sin/Issues/Problems

We end where we began…

Christ came to redeem not only us but also all of Creation!

Christ's prophetic warning in Matthew 7:21–23 has everything to do with a _____ relationship with Him that is then lived out and observed by the world in our relationships, first in our families and then in His Church.

We must truly _____ by His grace through faith (Ephesians 2:8-9), then strive to live out this _____ relationship with Him (Philippians 2:12-13).

This gives us His Authority in the lives of others as they will see it and invite us to have influence in their lives—True Authority lived out in Love!

> *Who will stand for the Truth about right, good, and morality?*
> *That is who will either make a difference or be*
> *persecuted for trying and in the end will be proven right!*

Living in God's Covenant Design

God's design always moves from the individual to the relational (marriage and family) into the community (Church) and finally into systems (governments).

When we fail to make strong _____ in loving _____ in our homes, then the best we can do, even with the greatest of intentions, is create a façade of loving community and systems that will ultimately enslave.

Even our churches then become primarily a system of _____ and _____ rather than a loving and united fellowship of believers.

That's why God began with a _____ and a family!

The Truth of His Love and Lordship has never changed.

> *"There is only one relationship that matters, and that is your personal relationship to a personal Redeemer and Lord. Let everything else go, but maintain that at all costs, and God will fulfil His purpose through your life. One individual life may be of priceless value to God's purposes, and yours may be that life."*
>
> — Oswald Chambers, *My Utmost for His Highest*

NOTES

Fill-in-the-blank Answers

SECTION 1

P. 6 – reflect; separated; control; feeling; lording it; worldly

P. 7 – Author; Father; Son; Word; Truth; Order

P. 8 – submit; Truth; firm; faith

P. 9 – everything; lordship; leadership; different; One; Only; worship; command; marriage/family; Church

P. 10 – rule; others; authority; expecting; lose; confident; content; modeled

P. 11 – intimate; headship/authority

P. 12 – Character; our leaders

SECTION 2

P. 15 – priorities; Lord/lord; master; control; deceptions; feelings/emotions

P. 16 – Truth; Commitment; True confidence; Lead by example; shalom, integer; student/servant; disciple; student-servants; always

P. 17 - Confusion; liar; God/gods; kingdoms; Kings/two; Light; darkness; His Truth; deceived;
Path to The Fall and Sin blanks: Confusion; Deception; Touch; Taste; Indulge; Addiction/Bondage; determines

P. 18 – temptation; invited influence;

SECTION 3

P. 20 – WAY; Wholehearted; disciple

P. 21 – reveals; obedience-based; accountability; training; Submission; Surrender; Sacrifice; Service; SHAPE; sacrifice

P. 22 – full; complete; confident; Service; washing their feet; seperated; servant; Sacrificial; discipleship; Blessing

P. 23 – required; authority; love; daily; listening; thinking; fellowship

P. 24 – obedient; spiritual

SECTION 4

P. 28 – mammon/money; relationships; lived out; porneia/porn; first; eternal; priorities

P. 29 – Hesed; Agape; source

P. 30 – sexual immorality/sin; stronghold; willingly; battle; pursuit; minds; hearts

P. 31 – Self-focus; opens the door; change; self; nature; die; self; stronger

P. 32 – unconditional; intentional; full-orbed; compassion; Truth

P. 33 – Greatest; reflects; offspring; Priorities; decision-making; sacrifice; build loving relationships

NOTES

> *Richard John Neuhaus said it plainly:*
> *"If a church offers no truth that is not available in the general culture... there is not much reason to pay it attention."*

For more information and to
have Greg Williams speak at your
church or organization, contact
Love & Lordship at
loveandlordship@gmail.com.

www.loveandlordship.com
On Facebook and Twitter
@LoveandLordship
Also on Apple Podcast, Google Play, YouTube and Vimeo

*Special thanks to Jeff Hancock for
the design and formatting of this workbook.*